Book 1
Excel Shortcuts

BY SAM KEY

&

Book 2
Rails Programming Professional Made Easy

BY SAM KEY

Book 1

Excel Shortcuts

BY SAM KEY

The 100 Top Best Powerful Excel Keyboard Shortcuts in 1 Day!

Programming Box Set #74: Excel Shortcuts & Rails Programming Professional Made Easy

Programming Box Set #74: Excel Shortcuts & Rails Programming Professional Made Easy

Table Of Contents

Introduction

I want to thank you and congratulate you for purchasing the book, "The Power of Excel Shortcuts: The 100 Top Best Powerful Excel Keyboard Shortcuts in 1 Day!".

This book contains proven steps and strategies on how to master the Microsoft Excel through just 100 keyboard shortcuts! However, most people will ask, "Why do you need to learn these shortcuts anyway?"

Advantages of Using Microsoft Excel

Microsoft Excel has become one of the most commonly used enterprise software in schools and offices. Its way of presenting data, which is through a spreadsheet, has helped a lot of people especially in the field of data mining. If you were going to put numerous rows of data, in let's say, a word processing program, it might take a lot of time creating tables and formatting each of them to fit in the pages. With the Microsoft Excel, these manual tasks are now much easier.

What does the Microsoft Excel have that other programs don't? For one, it has a built-in spreadsheet that you can manipulate the size and formatting. This versatile way of maneuvering the spreadsheet made it indispensable for many. Now, gone are the days were people have to manually draw tables in sheets of paper. Excel has already the tables prepared for them.

Another nifty feature of this software is its calculation function. Excel houses a myriad of formulas for solving arithmetic, financial and logical problems, among others. Thus, one doesn't even need to calculate every sum or average of a data series. Just by using a formula in Excel, everything can be done in an instant.

The Secret behind Mastering Excel

Speaking of instant, did you know that Excel has more than a hundred keyboard shortcuts? What does this mean to you as an Excel user? It means you can continuously work on your Excel spreadsheet without having to depend on your mouse constantly for Excel functions.

This is especially helpful whenever you are inputting a lot of data, and doing this will be more efficient if both of your hands weren't switching from keyboard to mouse and vice versa, every once in a while. In addition, if your mouse suddenly chose the most inopportune time to malfunction, learning Excel shortcuts can save you from major headaches.

As such, this book will provide you 100 keyboard shortcuts which you can use in Excel. In addition, as a bonus, you will learn about alternatives in case you forget any of these shortcuts.

Thanks again for purchasing this book, I hope you enjoy it!

Chapter 1: Moving Around the Excel Screen

People typically use the mouse for navigating the Excel screen. With this device, you can manipulate every cell in Excel, including its formatting and color. Since the mouse can access the major functions in Excel through the ribbon, there is no need for you to manually-type every formula or command.

However, the only difficult thing that you cannot do with a mouse is entering text. If you're going to use an on-screen keyboard, keying in the data in every cell would probably take you a lot longer than just using the keyboard for the text.

Thus, if you're going to use the keyboard most of the time, especially if you're just starting to build the spreadsheet data from scratch, it would be helpful to learn the basic keyboard shortcuts for moving around the Excel spreadsheet.

Shortcut #1: Arrow Keys

There are four arrow keys found in the right side of your main keyboard keys. These are the Arrow Left, Arrow Right, Arrow Up, and Arrow Down keys. Intuitively, you know that you can use these keys for moving within the spreadsheet. For instance, by selecting a cell then pressing Arrow Up, it will situate the cursor in the cell directly above your selected cell.

Shortcut #2: Ctrl + Arrow Key

Let's assume that you have a block of Excel data that spans more than 50,000 rows and more than 200 columns. You would probably have a hard time using a mouse in skimming these voluminous data. As such, you can use the Ctrl + Arrow key to navigate each "ends" of the data easily. In this example, click any cell in the block of data then press Ctrl + Arrow Down. You will be immediately located to the bottom cell in that specific column.

Shortcut #3: Shift + Arrow Key

You have selected all the items in the row but you forgot to include one cell. What would you do if you needed to include the next cell in the selection? Simply press Shift + Arrow Key, where the arrow pertains to the direction of the region you want to highlight.

Shortcut #4: Ctrl + Shift + Arrow Key

The above shortcut only includes one cell in the selection; but what would happen if you want to include everything until the last cell containing a data? You then use the Ctrl + Shift + Arrow Key.

Shortcut #5: Backspace

The Backspace key immediately deletes the contents of the active cell. However, if the cell is in Edit mode, it will only delete one character in the left of the insertion point, or the blinking cursor in the Formula bar.

Shortcut #6: Delete

This key has the same function as the Backspace key. However, instead of the left side, it removes a character in the right hand side of the insertion point.

Shortcut #7: End

Pressing the End key will enable the End Mode in Excel. In this mode, if you press an Arrow key, it will directly take you to the last used cell (or if none, last cell) in that specific direction. However, if the Scroll Lock is on, pressing the End key will only take you to the lower right corner of your Excel screen.

Shortcut #8: Ctrl + End

It works the same as the End key where pressing this combination will take you to the last used cell. However, if no cells were used, it will not move to the end of the worksheet like the End key does. Also, if the insertion point is located in the Formula bar (e.g., after the first character), Ctrl + End will put this cursor at the end of the field.

Shortcut #9: Ctrl + Shift + End

This keyboard shortcut can do two functions. First, in the Formula bar, it will select every character at the right of the insertion point. On the other hand, if you use it in the worksheet, it will highlight the cells starting from the active cell (or selected cell) until the last used cell in the worksheet.

Shortcut #10: Spacebar

Aside from putting a space in your text, it can also either select or clear a checkbox.

Shortcut #11: Ctrl + Spacebar

This will select the whole column to where the active cell is located.

Shortcut #12: Shift + Spacebar

It has the same function as the above, but this shortcut selects rows instead of columns.

Shortcut #13: Ctrl + Shift + Spacebar

Pressing these keys will select your entire worksheet.

Shortcut #14: Enter

After you have entered a data in a cell, pressing the Enter key will complete the input of data. Besides that, you can also directly go one cell below through this key. Considered as the most commonly used shortcut in Excel, you will be using the Enter key quite a lot because all Excel functions need it.

Shortcut #15: Shift + Enter

If you press Enter, you will go down one cell. Conversely, a Shift + Enter will complete an entry in a cell but the cursor will go directly above your entry.

Shortcut #16: Ctrl + Enter

Since this is a spreadsheet, it follows that after you have put an entry, you will enter another data below it. That is the common task whenever you're working on a table or database, which explains why the Enter key goes down. However, if you think that you need the downward movement, you can try Ctrl + Enter. This will plainly enter your data in the cell and it won't move your cursor to another direction.

Shortcut #17: Alt + Enter

You want the data to go into the next line in the same cell. However, if you press Enter, the cursor just moves on to the next cell in line. Pressing the Tab key doesn't work either. So what will you do? Try Alt + Enter key and see if it works.

Shortcut #18: Esc Key

The Escape key, or simply "Esc", performs a lot of nifty functions in Excel. Among of which are the following: 1) deletes a whole data in a cell, 2) exits you from a dialog box, and 3) escapes you from the full screen mode of Excel.

Shortcut #19: Home Key

The Home key will take you to the first cell in the specific row of your active cell. However, if the Scroll Lock is on, the cursor will go to the upper-left corner of your current window.

Shortcut #20: Ctrl + Home

This shortcut, also known as the "True Home key", brings the user to the beginning of the worksheet.

Shortcut #21: Ctrl + Shift + Home

This will select all cells from the active cell up to the first cell in the worksheet.

Shortcut #22: Page Down

Scouring among rows and rows of worksheets is now easy because of this button. This will display the next page in your Excel window.

Shortcut #23: Alt + Page Down

Unlike Page Down, the Alt + Page Down combination will show the next page to the right of your current window.

Shortcut #24: Ctrl + Page Down

Flipping in several worksheets is now easy thanks to Ctrl + Page Down. This will automatically turn you over to the next worksheet.

Shortcut #25: Ctrl + Shift + Page Down

The normal way of selecting several worksheets at once is to hold Ctrl while clicking each of the worksheets to be included in the selection.

However, for those who don't think this is the practical way to do it, here's an alternative. Use the Ctrl + Shift + Page Down; it will automatically select the sheets for you.

Shortcut #26: Page Up

This is quite similar to Shortcut #22: Page Down key, except for the fact that this one goes in the opposite direction (which is upward).

Shortcut #27: Alt + Page Up

The Alt + Page Up will move your screen to the left, instead of right as what was described in Shortcut #23: Alt + Page Down.

Shortcut #28: Ctrl + Page Up

Same as Shortcut #24: Ctrl + Page Down, this will enable you to change sheets easily. However, this one goes in a counterclockwise direction.

Shortcut #29: Ctrl + Shift + Page Up

Selecting sheets is also a function of the Ctrl + Shift + Page Up. However, it will select the worksheets on the left hand side of your current sheet first.

Shortcut #30: Tab Key

Using the Tab key will enable you to move to the right hand side of the cell. Also, if you have a protected worksheet, pressing this can immediately take you to the next unlocked cell. Lastly, in case there is a dialog box, you can easily move along the options through the Tab key.

Shortcut #31: Shift + Tab

The Shift + Tab works the opposite way; if pressing Tab will take you to the right hand cell, this shortcut will locate the left cell for you. It also applies to the other functions of the Tab key. In a dialog box for instance, keying in Shift + Tab will move you to the previous option.

Shortcut #32: Ctrl + Tab

You're now done with shortcuts for moving around cells and worksheets. As such, the succeeding shortcuts in this chapter will focus on dialog boxes. For this shortcut, use it if you want to go to the next tab in a dialog box.

Shortcut #33: Ctrl + Shift + Tab

However, if you wish to go back to the previous tab in a dialog box, using the Ctrl + Shift + Tab is the right combination.

So there you have it, the first 33 keyboard shortcuts in Excel. Hopefully, through these tips you can know traverse in your multitude of cells and worksheets with no difficulty at all.

Chapter 2: Navigating the Excel Ribbon

Microsoft created the "ribbon" as a replacement to the expanding menus in the earlier versions of Microsoft Excel. It houses all the functions in Excel such as formatting, page layout, pictures, and shapes. However, since its interface is not in an expanding menu style, people are not that familiar with its keyboard shortcuts as compared to before where you can immediately see which shortcut runs which.

To help you with that, here are some of the most commonly used keyboard shortcuts for exploring the Ribbon.

Shortcut #34: Alt Key

Letters and numbers will appear in the ribbon once you push the Alt key. What happens is that it activates the access keys, wherein typing in corresponding letter or number will let you select a specific function in the ribbon.

Shortcut #35: F10

This key has the same function as the Alt key, only that pressing the F10 would require you to use your right hand instead.

Shortcut #36: Alt + Arrow Left/Right

To be able to navigate to the other tabs, use these keys.

Shortcut #37: F10 + Arrow Left/Right

Since it was previously mentioned that the F10 behaves the same way as the Alt key, pressing F10 followed by an arrow to the left or to the right will also transfer you to other tabs.

Shortcut #38: Ctrl + F1

There's no doubt that the ribbon indeed takes up quite a lot of space in your screen. Therefore, for those who want more area for their spreadsheet, hiding the ribbon is the best option. To do that, simply press Ctrl + F1. To show the ribbon again, also press the same shortcut.

Shortcut #39: Shift + F10

Shift + F10 is similar to the right click button of your mouse. It can open menus and other options depending on where your cursor is.

Shortcut #40: F6

You can move along three areas of the screen through this key. The F6 key, will take you either to the ribbon, the spreadsheet, or the status bar.

Shortcut #41: F10 + Tab

In a tab, you can browse through the functions by pressing this combination continuously. You can also press this shortcut first, and then proceed with the arrow keys for navigation.

Shortcut #42: F10 + Shift + Tab

The above shortcut goes around the functions in a clockwise manner. On the contrary, the F10 + Shift + Tab shortcut does otherwise.

Shortcut #43: F1

In the upper right corner of the ribbon, there is a blue question mark icon. Accessing this icon will take you to the Microsoft Excel Help task pane. Alternatively, if you press F1 the same pane will open.

Since the area around the ribbon is limited, it is only appropriate that there would be less keyboard shortcuts dedicated for it. All in all, there are ten button combinations for the ribbon.

Chapter 3: Formatting the Excel Spreadsheet

If you're also a user of the Microsoft Word, you are probably familiar with formatting keyboard shortcuts such as Ctrl + B, which stands for bold text or Ctrl + I, which italicizes your text. Since you can do almost every basic feature that you need in the Word application through the keyboard, this makes the formatting easier for you.

Fortunately, even though Excel is not a word-processing program, it also has dedicated keyboard shortcuts that for formatting. These are as follows:

Shortcut #44: Alt + '

By going to the Styles group in the Home tab, you can quickly change the appearance of the cell by selecting any of the pre-installed styles in Excel. To see the formatting changes done within a cell, you click on the New Style option, which will take you to the Style dialog box. Similarly, clicking Alt + ' will get you in the same menu.

Shortcut #45: Ctrl + B

Like in Microsoft Word, Ctrl + B will either apply or remove a bold format in a text.

Shortcut #46: Ctrl + 2

This shortcut can also make the selected text into a bold type.

Shortcut #47: Ctrl + I

Letter I stands for Italics. As such, clicking Ctrl + I will turn any text into an italicized type.

Shortcut #48: Ctrl + 3

This also functions like the Ctrl + I shortcut.

Shortcut #49: Ctrl + U

Ctrl + U will put an underline in the selected text.

Shortcut #50: Ctrl + 4

Another alternative for the Ctrl +U is the Ctrl + 4 shortcut.

Shortcut #51: Ctrl + 5

To easily put a strikethrough in your text, press Ctrl + 5.

Shortcut #52: Ctrl + Shift + F

If you want more font formatting options, you can just proceed to the Font tab of the Format cells dialog box. Right-clicking a cell then selecting Format Cells will get you there, or you can just use this shortcut.

Shortcut #53: Ctrl + Shift + P

This shortcut works the same as the above.

Shortcut #54: Ctrl + Shift + &

Now that you're done with editing the text, this shortcut as well as the succeeding ones will pertain to cell formatting. As for Ctrl + Shift + &, it will put a plain black border on all sides of the cell.

Shortcut #55: Ctrl + Shift + _

On the contrary, Ctrl + Shift + _ will remove the borders that you have made.

Shortcut #56: F4

Instead of manually doing all the formatting for a number of cells, Excel has a shortcut wherein you can redo the formatting that you just did in another cell. This is the F4 function key. For example, if you have put borders in Cell A1, selecting Cell A2 then pressing F4 will also create borders for that specific cell.

Shortcut #57: Ctrl + 1

Pressing the Ctrl + 1 will show the Format Cells dialog box. In this box, you can edit every possible formatting for a cell such as number format, alignment, font, border, and fill.

The previous chapters have discussed how certain shortcuts can perform specific functions in Excel such as formatting cells and navigating the spreadsheet. In the following chapters, the topics will be about the different uses of specific buttons such as the Function keys and the Control key.

Chapter 4: Working with Function Keys

The first row of keys in your keyboard contains the function keys, which is denoted by the letter F followed by a number. In the Windows desktop, these function keys can do a variety of tasks such as adjusting the screen brightness or minimizing the volume.

Excel uses the function keys for different purposes. Thus, most people usually have a difficulty mastering the Function key shortcuts in Excel.

Shortcut #58: Alt + F1

Alt + F1 will automatically create a chart for you. Just select the range of cells containing your chart data then press this shortcut. Afterwards, a column chart will appear in the worksheet.

Shortcut #59: Alt + Shift + F1

The normal way in creating a new worksheet is by right-clicking any of the existing worksheets then choosing Insert. The same task can be done by this shortcut.

Shortcut #60: F2

In editing a formula, you can't just simply select an active cell; you have to click on the Formula bar so that you can make changes to it. Fortunately, the F2 will put the cell in Edit mode. Thus, if you want to amend a cell, there's no need for you to click on the Formula bar; just use F2 instead.

Shortcut #61: Shift + F2

The Shift + F2 shortcut will insert comments in the active cell.

Shortcut #62: Ctrl + F2

Unlike the previous F2 combinations, this one has nothing to do with editing a cell. When you press Ctrl + F2, you will be forwarded to the Print Preview screen. Upon exiting this screen, your spreadsheet will show dotted lines which serves as a marker for a page border.

Shortcut #63: F3

Instead of constantly referring to a range of cells by their cell location (e.g., A1:D1), you can just define a name for this range. Thus, whenever you want to pertain to that specific range in a formula, you can simply put its name; there's no need for you to put the cell range. F3 will take you to the Paste Name dialog box, wherein you can list all the names created in a worksheet and their respective cell references.

Shortcut #64: Ctrl + F3

To create a new name, go to the Name Manager through Ctrl + F3.

Shortcut #65: Shift + F3

Using formulas is the heart of Microsoft Excel. Without it, you cannot do any calculations in the spreadsheet. As such, there is a dedicated tab for Formulas in the Excel ribbon. However, it may take quite a lot of time for users to efficiently look for the appropriate formula with all the possible options in the Formulas tab. Because of this, the Shift + F3 key combination is made. It opens the Insert Function dialog box, wherein you can easily search for a formula by just typing in the description of what you need to do.

Shortcut #66: Ctrl + F4

You don't need to click that "X" mark in the upper left corner of your Excel screen just to close the application; a simple Ctrl + F4 is enough to do the job.

Shortcut #67: F5

Rummaging through a lot of cells takes a lot of work, especially if you're dealing with thousands of rows in a spreadsheet. The Go To dialog box, which can be accessed through F5, will help you reach that specific cell or range that you wanted to see.

Shortcut #68: Ctrl + F5

By default, all workbooks are always in full screen mode in Excel. However, if you're doing work on several Excel files at once, it may be hard to switch from one file to the other when each workbook is on full screen. Through Ctrl + F5, the selected file restore to window size in the Excel screen so that you can easily switch across files.

Shortcut #69: Shift + F6

This works the same as Shortcut #40: F6, albeit in a counterclockwise direction.

Shortcut #70: Ctrl + F6

If you have more than one workbook open, pressing Ctrl + F6 will let you switch among these workbooks.

Shortcut #71: F7

Aside from Microsoft Word, the Excel application has also a built-in spell checker. To check the spelling of every word in your spreadsheet, press F7. This will run the Spelling dialog box. Apart from detecting erroneous spellings, it also suggests possible words that can replace the incorrect word.

Shortcut #72: Ctrl + F7

As mentioned before, you should not use the full screen mode when working with several Excel files. This is so that you can select each workbook with ease. The Ctrl + F7 shortcut executes the Move command so that you can drag the unneeded workbooks in another area in the Excel screen where it can't obstruct your view.

Shortcut #73: F8

Upon pressing F8, the Excel goes into an Extend Selection mode. This enables you to use the arrow keys to extend the current selection. Pressing the same key will also lift the Extend Selection mode.

Shortcut #74: Shift + F8

The limitation of the F8 key is that it only adds adjacent cells in the selection. Through Shift + F8, you can now add any nonadjacent cell by using arrow keys.

Shortcut #75: Ctrl + F8

To resize your workbook, use Ctrl + F8. This will run the Size command for workbooks that are not in a full screen mode.

Shortcut #76: Alt + F8

A macro is a set of actions created using the Visual Basic programming language. What it does is to automate a set of tasks in Excel. For example, you're going to retrieve a data in a one sheet then you'll paste the said data in another sheet. However, if you're going to do the copy-paste task for thousands of data, it might take you a long time. As such, you can use the macro for this. Alt + F8 will open the Macro dialog box, where you can record and run a macro.

Shortcut #77: F9

This is the Refresh button in Excel. Once you refresh a workbook, it will recalculate all new formulas in the said file.

Shortcut #78: Shift + F9

On the other hand, Shift + F9 will only recalculate the formulas in the worksheet you are currently working on.

Shortcut #79: Ctrl + Alt + F9

This has the same function as F9, but it will also recalculate formulas that have not been changed.

Shortcut #80: Ctrl + Alt + Shift + F9

Aside from doing what the Ctrl + Alt + F9 shortcut does, it also rechecks all dependent formulas for any errors.

Shortcut #81: Alt + Shift + F10

Smart tags are data that are labeled in a particular type. For instance, a person's name in an Outlook email message can be labeled with this tag. You can open the smart tag menu through this shortcut.

Shortcut #82: Ctrl + F10

This will enable a workbook to display in full screen mode (or maximized mode).

Shortcut #83: F11

The Shortcut #58: Alt + F1 will let you create charts by highlighting the data series. Similarly, the F11 key has the same function except that you don't need to select the data series; it will automatically detect the data for you. Another difference between these two shortcuts is that the Alt + F1 will display the chart in the same worksheet, while the F1 key will make another worksheet for the new chart.

Shortcut #84: Shift + F11

This is an alternative to Shortcut #59: Alt + Shift + F1, wherein it will insert a new worksheet.

Shortcut #85: Alt + F11

Alt + F11 will open the Microsoft Visual Basic Editor. In this menu, you can create or edit a macro by using the Visual Basic for Applications (VBA) programming language.

Shortcut #86: F12

The F12 key is the shortcut for the Save As dialog box. It lets you save your Excel file among the available formats.

In case you're wondering why the F1, F4, F6 and F10 keys as well as some of their derivatives are not included in the list, these function keys have already been discussed in the previous chapters. Moreover, as this book specifically claims that it will contain at least a hundred keyboard shortcuts, putting these function keys again in the list will not create an accurate count of all the shortcuts.

Chapter 5: Discovering Ctrl Combinations

There are more than 50 Ctrl key combinations that you can use in the Excel sheet, with some shortcuts comprising of special characters instead of the usual alphanumeric ones. Thus, it would be unpractical to include every possible shortcut, especially if there's a little chance that a typical user will use them all.

With these reasons, only the f14 most valuable Ctrl shortcuts will be contained in the list below.

Shortcut #87: Ctrl + ;

Ctrl + ; will show the current date in the active cell.

Shortcut #88: Ctrl + Shift + #

Ctrl + Shift + # will change the date into a day-month-year format.

Shortcut #89: Ctrl + A

This is an alternative to Shortcut #13: Ctrl + Shift + Spacebar. Pressing these keys will also select the whole worksheet.

Shortcut #90: Ctrl + C

Ctrl + C will copy the contents of the active cell.

Shortcut #91: Ctrl + F

If you need to search for a specific data, you don't have to go to the Home tab and choose Find & Select. By pressing Ctrl + F, you can now access the Find and Replace dialog box immediately.

Shortcut #92: Ctrl + K

To insert or edit a hyperlink, use this shortcut.

Shortcut #93: Ctrl + R

This activates the Fill Right command. To use this, simply click on a cell you want filled then press Ctrl + R. It will copy all the formatting and contents of the cell to its left.

Shortcut #94: Ctrl + S

Ctrl + S will automatically save your file in its current name, location and format.

Shortcut #95: Ctrl + V

After doing Shortcut #90: Ctrl + C, you then proceed with Ctrl + V to paste the contents that you have copied.

Shortcut #96: Ctrl + Alt + V

Since the above shortcut will paste all the data as is, the Ctrl + Alt + V will give you most pasting options as it will open the Paste Special dialog box.

Shortcut #97: Ctrl + W

This combination is an alternative to Shortcut #66: Ctrl + F4, which closes the Excel program.

Shortcut #98: Ctrl + X

This will cut the contents of an active cell. When you say "cut", it will remove the data in a cell and will place it temporarily in the Clipboard so that you can paste the contents in another cell.

Shortcut #99: Ctrl + Y

The Ctrl + Y shortcut runs the Redo function, which means that it will repeat the previous command that you have done.

Shortcut #100: Ctrl + Z

Lastly, Ctrl + Z serve as the shortcut for the Undo function. This will reverse your latest command in Excel.

And that finishes our countdown for the Top 100 keyboard shortcuts in Microsoft Excel. To wrap things up, the last chapter will provide some pointers in "memorizing" these shortcuts the easiest way.

Chapter 6: Pointers for the Excel Novice

Most people will most likely feel daunted with the mere volume of shortcuts in this book. "How can I ever memorize a hundred of these combinations?", says most people. This fear of memorization only impedes the learning process. As such, you should stay away from this negative thinking.

Practice a Couple of Shortcuts Every Week

To be able to remember these shortcuts effectively, you should use them as often as you could. Have this book by your side always so that you will have a guide as you try to absorb each of these shortcuts. Better yet, you can jot down a couple of shortcuts in a small list so that you can try some of these tricks in your school or the office.

After finishing let's say at least five shortcuts for a week, add another five in the succeeding weeks. Just don't forget the previous shortcuts that you have learned. In no time, you will be able to use these keyboard combinations without the help of a cheat sheet.

Don't Use the Numeric Keypad

Although most people on the go use laptops such as students, many people still use the full-sized keyboard that has a built-in numeric keypad at the right side.

Although several characters in the listed shortcuts are there, the Microsoft Excel does not recognize the use of numeric keypad in its shortcuts. As such, you shouldn't try to practice these shortcuts via the numeric keypad; just use the main keyboard itself.

That ends all the pointers in this guide for Excel shortcuts. With that, you should apply all the learnings that you have discovered through this book in your daily Excel tasks. Hopefully, you'll be a more efficient Excel user as you incorporate these shortcuts in using the said spreadsheet program.

Conclusion

Thank you again for purchasing this book!

I hope this book was able to help you to learn the secrets behind mastering Microsoft Excel, which are the 100 keyboard shortcuts.

The next step is to make use of these shortcuts every time you operate on the Excel application. Through this, you can now easily work on your Excel spreadsheets with only a minimal use of a mouse.

Finally, if you enjoyed this book, please take the time to share your thoughts and post a review on Amazon. We do our best to reach out to readers and provide the best value we can. Your positive review will help us achieve that. It'd be greatly appreciated!

Thank you and good luck!

Book 2
Rails Programming Professional Made Easy

BY SAM KEY

Expert Rails Programming Success In A Day For Any Computer User!

Programming Box Set #74: Excel Shortcuts & Rails Programming Professional Made Easy

Table Of Contents

Introduction

I want to thank you and congratulate you for purchasing the book, "insert book title here Professional Rails Programming Made Easy: Expert Rails Programming Success In A Day For Any Computer User!"

This book contains proven steps and strategies on how to learn the program Ruby on Rails and immediately create an application by applying the rudiments of this platform.

Rails is one of the newest and most popular platforms. Thanks to the growth of Internet, this platform has been targeting audiences that are quite interested in creating stable web designs. If your work involves the Internet and you want to implement ideas that would help you launch projects online, you would definitely want to learn how to code using this program. Within this book are everything that you need to learn from installing the platform, getting the basics and making sure that you are ready to rock any programmer's boat.

Thanks again for purchasing this book. I hope you enjoy it!

Chapter 1 Why Rails Matters

If you are a computer programmer, the Ruby on Rails platform would probably the next program that you have to learn how to use. It is also worth looking into if your work is largely based on design, and you want to try something current to make websites easy to manipulate and beautiful. It could also be the platform that would launch your career or create leverage for yourself at the office. Yes, this platform could be your trump card to your next promotion, or that awesome site that you have in mind.

What Rails Can Do For You

If you are wondering what good this program can do for most computer users, then here are the awesome things that you can get out of the platform.

1. Get to Code

Coding is not rocket science, and if you are using Ruby, you probably would not even feel that you are using a programming language. You would want to learn to code to retain what you are going to experience with the platform, so take the time to study anyway.

If you are getting into Rails, you do not need to be a Computer Science major. If you are a businessman who has a great idea for a web app and you want to try coding it yourself, then this platform may be your best bet.

2. Get to Code Better

Sometimes it is not about arguing what is the best platform out there and get drunk arguing which is the best among Python, Java, PHP, or Ruby. If you already know other programming languages, you would need to still keep up with the times and learn some new tricks. Ruby on Rails provides that opportunity.

3. Get to Code Faster

RoR is a beautiful platform that allows you to write shorter codes, and it has a great set of features for exception handling which makes it really easy to spot and handle possible errors. You also would not need to still maintain the usual reference counts in your extension libraries. You also get awesome support using Ruby from C, which gives you better handle when you want to write C extensions.

RoR makes any programmer productive because it is opinionated and it gives guesses on how you can probably code something in the best way possible. The Don't Repeat Yourself (DRY) Principle of RoR also makes you skip the usual coding process of writing something again and again, which often makes the code long, complex, and difficult to debug. That means that at the end of the project, you get to look at your code and have a better grasp of what happened there.

4. Understand How Twitter Works

Yes, Twitter is created using RoR, and if you are an SEO specialist, a web designer, or simply a tech geek, knowing how this social media platform is done would definitely help you out. You would also discover that a lot of the hot new websites today are built on this platform.

5. Learn a Platform with a Great Community

RoR is relatively young compared to other programming languages, and for that reason, it has a very active and collaborative community. You definitely would get to hang out with several other developers and would probably build something together. Doing that is always good for your résumé.

6. It works with all operating systems and offers threading that is independent from the operating system. That means that is also very portable, and would even work on a computer that runs on Windows 95.

If these perks sound great, then it's time to get started with a Rails project!

Chapter 2 Getting Started

If you want to learn how to use Rails, then you would need to first have the following:

1. Ruby – choose the language version that is 1.9.3, or later. You can download it by visiting ruby-lang.org.

2. RubyGems packaging system – it is typically installed with Ruby that has versions 1.9 or newer.

3. Installed SQLite3 Database

Rails, as you probably figured out, is a framework dedicated to web application development written in the language of Ruby. That means that you would want to learn a little bit of Ruby coding in order to eliminate any difficulty in jumping into Rails. If you have a browser open, you can get great help in practicing Ruby codes by logging in to tryruby.org, which features a great interactive web tutorial. Try it out first to get the hang out of coding with Ruby.

If you do not have any working SQLite 3 yet, you can find it at sqlite.org. You can also get installation instructions there.

Installing Rails

1. Run the Rails installer (for Windows and Mac users) or the Tokaido (Mac OS X users)

2. Check out the version of the installed Ruby on your computer by running the Run command on Start menu and then typing cmd on the prompt (Windows). If you are running on Mac OS X, launch Terminal.app.

Key in "$ ruby –v" (no captions). After you hit Enter, you will see the Ruby version installed

3. Check out the version of SQLite3 installed by typing "$ sqlite3 –version".

4. After Rails installation, type in "$ rails –version" on Terminal.app or at the command prompt. If it says something similar to Rails 4.2.0, then you are good to go.

A Note on the $ sign

The $ sign would be used here in this book to look like the terminal prompt where you would type your code after. If you are using Windows for the Rails platform, you would see something like this: c:\source_code> .

Chapter 3 Create Your First Project

Here's something that most web developers are raving about Rails: it comes with generators, or scripts that are made to make development a lot easier by making all things that you need to get started on a particular project. Among these scripts is the new application generator, which gives you the foundation you need for a new Rails app so you do not have to write one yourself. Now that allows you to jump right into your code!

Since you are most likely to build a website or an API (application program interface), you would want to start coding a blog application. To start, launch a terminal and go to any directory where you can create files. On the prompt, type "$ rails new blog."

After you hit Enter, Rails will start making an application called Blog in the directory. It will also start making gem dependencies that you already have in your Gemfile bundle install.

Now, go to where your blog app is by typing in "$ cd blog".

What's in There?

Once you get into the directory, you will find a number of files that Rails have already installed by default. If you are not quite sure about what these files are for, here's a quick rundown of the file or folder functions:

1. app/ - this has the models, helpers, mailers, assets, and controllers for the app you just created. You'll be looking more at this folder later.

2. bin/ - this has the script that you will use to run the app. Also, this has other scripts that you will be using to deploy, setup, or run the application you are going to create.

3. config/ - this allows you to tweak the app's database, routes, etc.

4. config.ru – this is the configuration that will be used by Rack-based servers to run the app.

5. db/ - this would contain your database and database migrations

6. Gemfile, Gemfile.lock – these would allow you to tell the program what sort of gem dependencies you are going to need for the app you're building.

7. lib/ - contains the extended modules needed for the app

8. lib – contains the app's log files

9. public/ – this would be the sole folder that other people could see. It would be containing all your compiled assets and created static files.

10. Rakefile – this would be the one file that would locate and load tasks that can be set to run from the command line. You can add tasks that you would prefer to use later on by adding the files needed to the lib/tasks directory

11. README.rdoc – just like readme's function, this would be a brief document that would tell other people how your app works, how to set it up, etc.

12. test/ - these would contain all your unit tests and all the things that you are going to need for testing.

13. tmp/ - this would hold all temporary files

14. vendor/ - this would contain all your third-party codes and would also contain all vendored gems.

Now, if you are seeing all these in the app directory you just made, then you are ready to create little bits and pieces that you would be adding up later to make a real blog app!

Firing Up the Web Server

Since you already have the barebones of your blog application, you would want to set up how the app is going to be launched on the internet. To start a web server go to the directory where blog is located, and then type "$ bin/rails server".

Important note:

You would need to have a JavaScript runtime available in your computer if you want to use asset compression for JavaScript or if you want to compile a CoffeeScript. Otherwise, you would expect to see an execjs error when you attempt to compile these assets. If you want to look at all the supported runtimes, you can go to github.com/sstephenson/execjs#readme.

If you are successful, what you just did would launch WEBrick, which is the server that Ruby apps use by default. You can see what's happening so far in your app by firing up a web browser and typing http://localhost:3000. Now, since you have done nothing much, you would be seeing the Rails default page. It will tell you that you are currently in development mode. You also do not need to constantly require the server to look at the changes that you have made – any changes will be automatically picked up and seen. Also keep in mind that if you managed to see this "Welcome Aboard" thing, you are sure that you created an app that is configured correctly. If you want to find out the app's environment, click on "About your application's environment" link.

Got everything right so far? Let's move on to making something other people can read.

Chapter 4 Say "Hello There!"

If you want to make Rails learn how to say Hi to other people, you would need the following:

1. A controller

The purpose of a controller is to allow your program to receive any requests. When you route, you enable Rails to decide which of the controllers you set up will receive which types of requests. That may also mean that there would be different routes leading to the controller, which would be triggered by specific actions. An action is required in order to collect any information needed in order to send it to a view

2. A view

This thing's main purpose is to enable Rails to display the information made available to the action and display it in a format that other people can read. There are different view templates that are already available and coded using eRuby, which can be used in request cycles before it the information is sent to anyone who wants to look at this information.

Got it? Good. Now, to setup your welcome page, you need to generate a controller and then name it "welcome" using an action named "index". Your code will look like this:

$ bin/rails generate controller welcome index

Now, Rails will be creating a bunch of files plus a route for you to use. When Rails is done with that, you will see this:

```
create  app/controllers/welcome_controller.rb
 route  get 'welcome/index'
invoke  erb
create   app/views/welcome
create   app/views/welcome/index.html.erb
invoke  test_unit
create   test/controllers/welcome_controller_test.rb
invoke  helper
create   app/helpers/welcome_helper.rb
```

```
invoke  assets
invoke  coffee
create  app/assets/javascripts/welcome.js.coffee
invoke  scss
create  app/assets/stylesheets/welcome.css.scss
```

If you want to view where the course of your controller is, go to app/controllers/welcome_controller.rb. If you want to look at the view, you can find it at app/views/welcome/index.html.erb.

Here comes the fun part. Pull up a text editor and open app/views/welcome/index.html.erb there. Clear all the codes you see there, and replace it with this:

```
<h1>Hello Rails!</h1>
```

After doing so, you have successfully informed Rails that you want "Hello Rails!" to appear. That means that it is also the greeting that you want to see when you go to http://localhost:3000, which is still displaying "Welcome aboard".

Create the App's Home Page

The next thing that you need to do is to tell Rails where the home page is. To do that, pull up your text editor again and open config/routes.rb. You should see something like this:

```
Rails.application.routes.draw do
get 'welcome/index'

# The priority is based upon order of creation:
# first created -> highest priority.
#
# You can have the root of your site routed with "root"
# root 'welcome#index'
#
# ...
```

Those lines represent the routing file which tells Rails how to link requests to specific actions and controllers. Now, find the line "root 'welcome#index'" and uncomment it. When you get back to http://localhost:3000, you will see that it now displays Hello Rails!

Chapter 5 Let's Do Something More

Now that you have figured out how to make a controller, a view, and an action, it's time to create a new resource. A resource is something that groups together similar objects the same way you group people, plants, and animals. To make items for resources, you use the CRUD method (create, read, update, destroy).

Rails make it easy for you to build websites because it already comes with a method for resources that it can use for making a REST resource. REST, or Representational State Transfer is known as the web's architectural structure which is used to design all applications that use a network, and instead of using rather complex operations to link two machines, you can use HTTP to make machines communicate. That means that in a lot of ways, the Internet is based on a RESTful design.

Now, following the project you are creating, pull up config/routes.rb and make sure it's going to look like this:

```
Rails.application.routes.draw do

  resources :articles

  root 'welcome#index'
end
```

If you are going to look at the rake routes, you will notice that Rails has already made routes for all actions involving REST. It is going to look like this:

```
$ bin/rake routes
   Prefix        Verb                          URI          Pattern
Controller#Action
  articles GET   /articles(.:format)       articles#index
         POST  /articles(.:format)       articles#create
 new_article    GET                /articles/new(.:format)
articles#new
edit_article   GET              /articles/:id/edit(.:format)
articles#edit
   article GET   /articles/:id(.:format)     articles#show
```

PATCH /articles/:id(.:format) articles#update
PUT /articles/:id(.:format) articles#update
DELETE /articles/:id(.:format) articles#destroy
root GET / welcome#index

Chaper 6 Creating Article Title

This part would be the creating and reading part of CRUD, where you would put in a location where you would be placing articles for the blog you're building. In order to do so, you can create an ArticlesController by running this code:

```
$ bin/rails g controller articles
```

Now, you need to manually place an action inside the controller that you just created. Go to app/controllers/articles_controller.rb and pull up the class ArticlesController. Edit it to look like this:

```
class ArticlesController < ApplicationController

  def new

  end

end
```

You now have to create a template that Rails would be able to view. In order to create a title for the article that you want to display, pull up app/views/articles/new.html.erb and make a new file there. Type the following:

```
<h1>New Article</h1>
```

What did just happen? Check out http://localhost:3000/articles/new and you will see that the page now has a title! You will now want to create a template that will look like a form that you can fill up to write your articles in online.

Chapter 7 Creating the Form

Pull up app/views/articles/new.html.erb and then add this code:

```
<%= form_for :article do |f| %>
  <p>
    <%= f.label :title %><br>
    <%= f.text_field :title %>
  </p>

  <p>
    <%= f.label :text %><br>
    <%= f.text_area :text %>
  </p>

  <p>
    <%= f.submit %>
  </p>
<% end %>
```

You will see that you have just created a form that has a space for the article title text, submit button, and it comes with boxes too! That is the function of the code form_for. You will realize that when you submit an article you are going to create, it needs to be done in another URL and then the entire text should then go somewhere else. Edit app/views/articles/new.html.erb by finding the form_for line and make it look like this:

```
<%= form_for :article, url: articles_path do |f| %>
```

In Rails, the action “create” does the job of making new forms for submissions, and therefore, your form should be working towards this action. You would notice that when you try to submit an article, you would see an error there. In order to make it work, you need to make a “create action” within the ArticlesController.

Create the Article

In order to get rid of this error, you need to edit the ArticlesController class found in app/controllers/articles_controller.rb. It should look like this:

```
class ArticlesController < ApplicationController
    def new
    end

    def create
    end
end
```

Once that is done, the controller should now be able to save the article to the database. Now, you would need to set the parameters of actions done by controllers. Now, make the ending of the above lines to look like this instead:

```
def create
  render plain: params[:article].inspect
end
```

Now that should make the error go away. Try refreshing the page to see what happened.

Make the Model

Rails already provide a generator that would be used by your project to launch a model. To order Rails to start generating one, run this on the terminal:

```
$ bin/rails generate model Article title:string text:text
```

What just happened is that you told Rails that you are requiring an Article model that has a title and a text that are attributed to separate strings. You would see that the platform made up a lot of files, but you would be most interested in db/migrate/20140120191729_create_articles.rb which contains your blog's database.

Now, you would want to run a migration, which you can do with a single line of code:

$ bin/rake db:migrate

What Rails would do is that it would be executing this command which means that it made the Articles Table:

```
== CreateArticles: migrating ==================================================
-- create_table(:articles)
  -> 0.0019s
== CreateArticles: migrated (0.0020s) =========================================
```

Chapter 8 Save Your Data

Pull up app/controllers/articles_controller.rb and edit the "create" action into this:

```
def create
  @article = Article.new(params[:article])

  @article.save
  redirect_to @article
end
```

You're almost able to create an article! However, when you refresh the page, you would see a Forbidden Attributes Error, and would point you at the line @article – Article.new(params[:article]). The reason Rails is giving you a hard time is because it wants you to tell what parameters should be in your controller actions. That allows your program to be secure once you run it, and prevent it from assigning wrong controller parameters which can make your entire coded program crash.

To fix this, edit out the highlighted line in the error you just saw and change it into:

@article = Article.new(params.require(:article).permit(:title, :text))

Show Your Work

In order to make the page display your article, you can make use of the "show" action by adding it to app/controllers/articles_controller.rb. Add these following lines:

```
class ArticlesController < ApplicationController
  def show
    @article = Article.find(params[:id])
  end

  def new
  end
```

Now let's add some style. Create a new file named app/views/articles/show.html.erb and put in the following lines:

```
<p>
 <strong>Title:</strong>
 <%= @article.title %>
</p>

<p>
 <strong>Text:</strong>
 <%= @article.text %>
</p>
```

Refresh http://localhost:3000/articles/new and then you will see that you can create articles and display them!

Chapter 9 Make Your Articles Neat

Find a way to list all the articles that you are going to create in order to have an organized database. To do that, pull up app/controllers/articles_controller.rb and add the following lines to create a control.

```
class ArticlesController < ApplicationController
  def index
    @articles = Article.all
  end

  def show
    @article = Article.find(params[:id])
  end

  def new
  end
```

Now, to add a view, pull up app/views/articles/index.html.erb and then add the following lines:

```
<h1>Article List</h1>

<table>
  <tr>
    <th>Title</th>
    <th>Text</th>
  </tr>

  <% @articles.each do |article| %>
    <tr>
      <td><%= article.title %></td>
      <td><%= article.text %></td>
    </tr>
  <% end %>
</table>
```

Head over to http://localhost:3000/articles and you will see all the articles that you have made so far.

Tidy Up Some More with Links

You definitely need to create links for the articles that you have created so your readers can pull them up easily. To add links, open app/views/welcome/index.html.erb and then change it to look like this:

```
<h1>Hello, Rails!</h1>
<%= link_to 'My Blog', controller: 'articles' %>
```

Now, what if you want to add a link that would allow you to write a new article right away? All you need to do is to add the following lines to app/views/articles/index.html.erb to have a New Article link:

```
%= link_to 'New article', new_article_path %>
```

If you want to create a link to go back to where you were previously, add the following lines to the same file:

```
<%= form_for :article, url: articles_path do |f| %>
...
<% end %>

<%= link_to 'Back', articles_path %>
```

Chapter 10 Create Some Rules, Too

When you are creating a blog program, you do not want your users to accidentally submit a blank page, and then just land right back where they were without knowing what they did. Rails can help you make sure that doesn't happen by editing the app/models/article.rb file to look like this:

```
class Article < ActiveRecord::Base
  validates :title, presence: true,
            length: { minimum: 5 }
end
```

That means that the title should be at least 5 characters in order for the article to go through, otherwise it would not be saved. Now that this rule for your blog is in place, you need to show the blog user that something went wrong and that the form should be filled up properly. To do that, tweak the "create" and "new" actions in app/controllers/articles_controller.rb in order to look like this:

```
def new
  @article = Article.new
end

def create
  @article = Article.new(article_params)

  if @article.save
    redirect_to @article
  else
    render 'new'
  end
end

private
  def article_params
    params.require(:article).permit(:title, :text)
```

```
    end
```

What just happened is that you told Rails that if the user did not type in 5 characters in the Title field, it should show the blank form again to the user. That doesn't offer much help. In order to tell the user what went wrong, edit the app/controllers/articles_controller.rb file again and to cater the following changes:

```
def create
  @article = Article.new(article_params)

  if @article.save
    redirect_to @article
  else
    render 'new'
  end
end

def update
  @article = Article.find(params[:id])

  if @article.update(article_params)
    redirect_to @article
  else
    render 'edit'
  end
end

private
  def article_params
    params.require(:article).permit(:title, :text)
  end
```

Now, to show this to the user, tweak the app/views/articles/index.html.erb file and add the following lines:

```
<table>
  <tr>
    <th>Title</th>
```

```
    <th>Text</th>
    <th colspan="2"></th>
  </tr>

  <% @articles.each do |article| %>
    <tr>
      <td><%= article.title %></td>
      <td><%= article.text %></td>
      <td><%=   link_to   'Show',   article_path(article)
%></td>
      <td><%=  link_to  'Edit',  edit_article_path(article)
%></td>
    </tr>
  <% end %>
</table>
```

Chapter 11 Update Articles

You would expect your users to change their minds about the article that they just wrote and make some changes. This would involve the Update action in CRUD, which would prompt you to add an edit action in the ArticlesController and add this function between the “create” and “new” actions. It should look like this:

```
def new
  @article = Article.new
end

def edit
  @article = Article.find(params[:id])
end

def create
  @article = Article.new(article_params)

  if @article.save
    redirect_to @article
  else
    render 'new'
  end
end
```

To allow a view for this, create a file and name it app/views/articles/edit.html.erb and then put in the following lines:

```
<h1>Editing article</h1>

<%= form_for :article, url: article_path(@article),
method: :patch do |f| %>

  <% if @article.errors.any? %>
   <div id="error_explanation">
    <h2>
```

```
    <%= pluralize(@article.errors.count, "error") %>
prohibited
    this article from being saved:
   </h2>
   <ul>
    <% @article.errors.full_messages.each do |msg|
%>
     <li><%= msg %></li>
    <% end %>
   </ul>
  </div>
 <% end %>

 <p>
  <%= f.label :title %><br>
  <%= f.text_field :title %>
 </p>

 <p>
  <%= f.label :text %><br>
  <%= f.text_area :text %>
 </p>

 <p>
  <%= f.submit %>
 </p>

<% end %>

<%= link_to 'Back', articles_path %>
```

Now, you would need to create the "update" action in app/controllers/articles_controller.rb. Edit the file to look like this:

```
def create
 @article = Article.new(article_params)

 if @article.save
  redirect_to @article
```

```
   else
    render 'new'
   end
  end

  def update
   @article = Article.find(params[:id])

   if @article.update(article_params)
    redirect_to @article
   else
    render 'edit'
   end
  end

  private
   def article_params
    params.require(:article).permit(:title, :text)
   end
```

In order to show a link for Edit, you can edit app/views/articles/index.html.erb to make the link appear after the Show link.

```
<table>
 <tr>
  <th>Title</th>
  <th>Text</th>
  <th colspan="2"></th>
 </tr>

 <% @articles.each do |article| %>
  <tr>
   <td><%= article.title %></td>
   <td><%= article.text %></td>
   <td><%= link_to 'Show', article_path(article)
%></td>
   <td><%= link_to 'Edit', edit_article_path(article)
%></td>
  </tr>
```

```
 <% end %>
</table>
```

Now, to give chance for the user to Edit his work, add these lines to the template app/views/articles/show.html.erb:

```
...

<%= link_to 'Back', articles_path %> |
<%= link_to 'Edit', edit_article_path(@article) %>
```

Chapter 12 Destroy Some Data

No, it does not mean that you have to ruin the entire program you built. At this point, you would need to make provisions for the user to delete some of the articles that he wrote. Since you are creating a RESTful program, you would need to use the following route:

```
DELETE /articles/:id(.:format)     articles#destroy
```

This route makes it easy for Rails to destroy resources and you would need to make sure that it is placed before the protected or private methods. Let's add this action to the app/controllers/articles_controller.rb file:

```
def destroy
  @article = Article.find(params[:id])
  @article.destroy

  redirect_to articles_path
end
```

After doing so, you would notice that the ArticlesController in app/controllers/articles_controller.rb will now appear this way:

```
class ArticlesController < ApplicationController
  def index
    @articles = Article.all
  end

  def show
    @article = Article.find(params[:id])
  end

  def new
    @article = Article.new
  end

  def edit
    @article = Article.find(params[:id])
```

```
  end

  def create
    @article = Article.new(article_params)

    if @article.save
      redirect_to @article
    else
      render 'new'
    end
  end

  def update
    @article = Article.find(params[:id])

    if @article.update(article_params)
      redirect_to @article
    else
      render 'edit'
    end
  end

  def destroy
    @article = Article.find(params[:id])
    @article.destroy

    redirect_to articles_path
  end

  private
    def article_params
      params.require(:article).permit(:title, :text)
    end
end
```

Now, it's time for you to let the user know that they have this option. Pull up the app/views/articles/index.html.erb file and add the following lines:

```
<h1>Listing Articles</h1>
```

```
<%= link_to 'New article', new_article_path %>
<table>
 <tr>
  <th>Title</th>
  <th>Text</th>
  <th colspan="3"></th>
 </tr>

 <% @articles.each do |article| %>
  <tr>
   <td><%= article.title %></td>
   <td><%= article.text %></td>
   <td><%= link_to 'Show', article_path(article)
%></td>
   <td><%= link_to 'Edit', edit_article_path(article)
%></td>
   <td><%= link_to 'Delete', article_path(article),
        method: :delete,
        data: { confirm: 'Are you sure?' } %></td>
  </tr>
 <% end %>
</table>
```

You would notice that you also added up a feature to make the user confirm whether he really would want to delete the submitted article. Now, in order to make the confirmation box appear, you need to make sure that you have the file jquery_ujs in your machine.

Conclusion

Thank you again for purchasing this book!

I hope this book was able to help you to grasp the basics of Ruby on Rails and allow you to create a webpage based on the codes and processes discussed in this book.

The next step is to discover other applications of the platform and learn other Rails techniques that would improve your program design and integration.

Finally, if you enjoyed this book, please take the time to share your thoughts and post a review on Amazon. We do our best to reach out to readers and provide the best value we can. Your positive review will help us achieve that. It'd be greatly appreciated!

Thank you and good luck!

Check Out My Other Books

Below you'll find some of my other popular books that are popular on Amazon and Kindle as well. Simply click on the links below to check them out. Alternatively, you can visit my author page on Amazon to see other work done by me.

C Programming Success in a Day

Python Programming Success in a Day

PHP Programming Professional Made Easy

HTML Professional Programming Made Easy

CSS Programming Professional Made Easy

Windows 8 Tips for Beginners

C Programming Professional Made Easy

JavaScript Programming Made Easy

C ++ Programming Success in a Day

Programming Box Set #74: Excel Shortcuts & Rails Programming Professional Made Easy

If the links do not work, for whatever reason, you can simply search for these titles on the Amazon website to find them.